For a better life
Love

A Book on Self-Empowerment

Compiled by
M. M. Walia

NEW DAWN PRESS, INC.
USA • UK • INDIA

NEW DAWN PRESS GROUP

Published by New Dawn Press Group
New Dawn Press, Inc., 244 South Randall Rd # 90, Elgin, IL 60123
e-mail: sales@newdawnpress.com

New Dawn Press, 2 Tintern Close, Slough, Berkshire, SL1-2TB, UK
e-mail: salesuk@newdawnpress.org

New Dawn Press (An Imprint of Sterling Publishers (P) Ltd)
A-59, Okhla Industrial Area, Phase-II, New Delhi-110020, India
e-mail: info@sterlingpublishers.com
www.sterlingpublishers.com

For a better life – Love

© 2006, Sterling Publishers (P) Ltd
ISBN 1 84557 578 4

All rights are reserved. No part of this publication may be reproduced, stored in a retrieval system or transmitted, in any form or by any means, mechanical, photocopying, recording or otherwise, without prior written permission of the publisher.

PRINTED IN INDIA

Love
The Greatest Commandment

"Love the
Lord your God
with all your heart,
with all your soul,
and with all your mind.
This is the greatest and
first commandment.
And the second is like it.
Love your neighbour
as yourself."
– The Bible

When love beckons to you,
follow him,
Though his ways are
hard and steep.
Like sheaves of corn
he gathers you unto himself.
He threshes you to make you naked,
He sifts you to free you from your husks.
He grinds you to whiteness.
He kneads you until you are pliant;
And then he assigns you to
his sacred fire, that you may
become sacred bread for
God's sacred feast.
– Kahlil Gibran

The Path of Devotion

He who with devotion offereth to Me a leaf, a flower, a fruit and water, that love-offering I accept, made by the pure-hearted.

Whatever thou doest, whatever thou eatest, whatever thou offerest as oblation, whatever thou givest and the austerities thou performest, do that as an offering to Me.

Thus wilt thou be freed from the bonds of action that beareth good and evil fruit, and thy soul, being engaged in this devotion of renunciation — liberated thou shalt come unto Me.

Alike am I to all beings, hated or beloved there is none to Me. But they who worship Me with devotion, in Me are they and in them am I.

— *The Bhagavad Gita*

Realising God

✦ If God's love is in your mind, you will see that nothing in the world is without this Love. When you love God, you will start seeing God among the animals, the trees, the inarticulate things. God is present even in that which we cannot see. Only the one who is absorbed in God recognises God's presence. Such a person has given his mind to God, and thus attains God. There is so much love in God that all the rivers — the whole universe — can be filled with it. The moment you touch God, you become filled with love.

✦ God is waiting at the gate, but all the gates are empty. No one is there to enter. So let us pass through that gate where love dwells, and only love.

— *Baba Virsa Singh Ji*

Love is Life

Love is like listening to a symphony; to be sensitive to the whole of that symphony. Can you imagine someone who is listening to the symphony and only hears the drum, or gives so much value to the drum that the other instruments are drowned out? A good musician who loves music will listen to them all. That is what love is, listening to the whole symphony, to be sensitive to all.

When the eyes are unobstructed, sight will emerge. When the heart is unobstructed of desires, attachments, obsessions — love will emerge.

Is it possible for a rose to say: I will give my fragrance to good people and withhold it from bad people? The rose, by its very nature, cannot but love all. Is it possible for a tree to say: I will give my shade to the good people and withhold it from the bad? It cannot. The tree gives shade even to the man who is striking it down, and if it is a tree with fragrance, it will leave its scent on the axe used to cut it!

What merit is yours if you only greet those who greet you and if you only love those who love you? You must be all loving, as your heavenly Father is all loving. He makes the sun shine on the good and bad alike and on the sin and the sinner.

— *Father Anthony de Mello*

A newly married couple asked: "What shall we do to make our love endure?"

Said the Master, "Love other things together."

— *Father Anthony de Mello*

> Power based on love is a thousand times more effective and permanent than the one derived from fear of punishment.
>
> – Mahatma Gandhi

Of the three varieties of love –
unselfish, selfish and mutual –
unselfish love is of the highest kind.
To love God is the essence of the whole
thing. Bhakti alone is the essence.
Love can only follow when there is respect.
Meditate on the power of Brahman –
all earthly creations are
manifestations of Brahman.
Brahman is *sat-chit-anand*.
Brahman is the ultimate perfection.

– Sri Ramakrishna Paramhans

The Path of Devotion

❖ Blessed are those who have devotion in their hearts. It is the only reality in the world, other things are false. Live a pure, holy life; be bold and fearless. Never mind if thousands fall before you; still stand firmly and never give up. Truly, what a great thing it is to have love and devotion! Devotion is the only thing which can make one happy.

❖ True devotion has wonderful powers. Through it a devotee can bring out divinity even from a stone. It is a living force and can give life to a dead body. They are indeed very happy who have naturally this devotion for the Lord. You know what Sri Ramakrishna says, — that the goal can be attained very easily through the power of faith and devotion, and never through the power of reasoning.

❖ It is true devotion that brings God-vision to us. No one can reach Him through mere intellect; nor even by the practice of Yoga or different kinds of hardships. This is the word of the Lord. He is to be attained by true and pure, unselfish and single-minded love. God is free. He is not bound by any law. Still He says "I remain bound to my devotees." As a great Saviour declared, "God is love and love is God." One can realise and feel this only with a sincere and pure heart. As long as we have selfish desires, we cannot expect to have this. It is holy and Divine.

❖ When this kind of love awakens, one becomes free from worldly ties. But we must not give up hope just because it is hard. However hard it may be from the standpoint of the world, still it must be realised. Without it the heart is but a barren ground. This is our life and this is the only reality in this world. And it is not at all hard for a sincere and true devotee, because his heart is made of love and naturally flows towards the Lord.

❖ It is through love that we feel the nearness or presence of the Divinity. Love unites God and man. When whole-hearted and simple-minded love for the Ideal awakens, it comes like a flood and washes off everything, — ignorance, narrowness, fear, doubt, selfishness — and leaves what? The Ideal.

❖ The Ideal alone is left shining in the heart. Then it becomes easy to renounce everything that is earthly, because nothing has any value except the Beloved. He is the Eternal, the Permanent, the Unchanging; all other things are transitory and changing. He is the Effulgent Spirit, everything else is perishable matter.

❖ When real devotion comes to the devotee, he grows humble and all-loving. The Beloved is all in all, he himself is nothing. Everywhere he sees his Beloved, therefore he becomes the servant of all; and through every living creature he serves his Ideal.

❖ So the true devotee worships his Ideal, not because he desires anything from him, but because He is dear to him, because He is his beloved whom he loves for the sake of love. So long as we expect something, we do not love truly, and the Ideal remains far from us. Only when we have begun to love for the sake of love are we truely devoted.

❖ Have true love for your Ideal, whatever you may call Him. Serve Him Faithfully.

- One must go into solitude to attain this Divine love. To get butter from milk you must let it set into curd in a secluded spot. If it is disturbed too much, the milk will not turn into curd. Next, you must put aside all other duties, sit in a quiet spot, and churn the curd. Only then, do you get butter. Similarly, by meditating on God in solitude, the mind acquires knowledge, dispassion and devotion.

- Pure knowledge and pure love are one and the same thing. Both lead the aspirants to the same goal. The path of love is much easier.

❖ Jnana is like a man, and Bhakti is like a woman. Knowledge has entry only up to the drawing-room of God, but Love can enter His inner apartments.

❖ Of all I could name, verily love is the highest — Love and devotion that make one forgetful of everything else. What ineffable joy does one find through love of me, the blissful Self. Once that joy is realised, all earthly pleasures fade into nothingness.

❖ Think not of self.

But let thy love encompass other hearts.

True love has no boundary lines;
Like the infinite sky it covers all space.

❖ He urged his countrymen to 'work like a master and not a slave'. He said: "Work through freedom! Work through love; The word 'love' is very difficult to understand; love never comes until there is freedom. There is no true love possible in a slave.

Every act of love brings happiness; there is no act of love which does not bring peace and blessedness as its reaction. Real existence, real knowledge, real love are eternally connected with one another, the three in one; where one of them is, the others also must be; they are the three aspects of the One without second — the Existence — Knowledge—Bliss."

❖ Love is the law of life. He who loves, lives, he who is selfish, is dying. Therefore, love for love's sake.

❖ In every nation the truth has been preached from most ancient times — love your fellow beings as yourselves. But no reason was forthcoming, no one knows why it would be good to love other beings as ourselves. And you understand why there is an impersonal God, when you learn that the whole world is one — that in hurting someone I am hurting myself, in loving someone I am loving myself. Hence, we understand why we ought not to hurt others.

❖ Love binds, love makes for that oneness — you become one, the mother with child, families with the city, the whole world becomes one. For love is existence, God Himself; and all this is the manifestation of that one love. The difference is only in degree, but it is the manifestation — of that one love — throughout. Nothing else is necessary but love, sincerity and patience. What is life, but growth, that is expansion, that is love. Therefore, all love is life. It is the only law of life; all selfishness is death and this is true here or hereafter.

— *From the writings of Swami Vivekananda and Swami Parmananda*

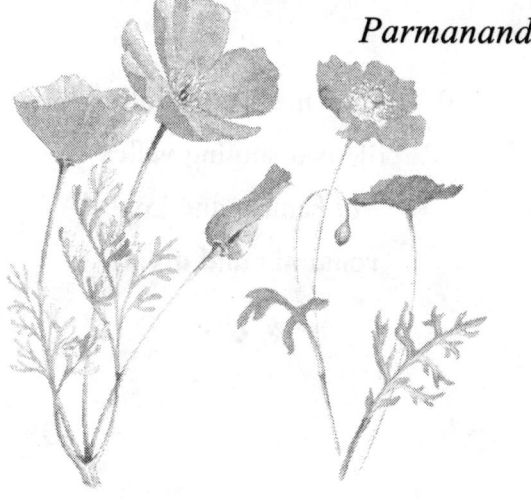

Swami Chinmayananda on Love

When our hearts are full of love,
life is a smiling valley
of beauty and joy,
romantic and divine.

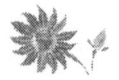

When love rises to swirl around us,
and when we re-view
in this clear light of love,
the very faults get transformed
into the essential beauty in them.
This is the magic touch of love,
the miracle played by love.

Love is not love,
if it does not serve and sacrifice.

We may often give without love,
   but we can never love without
            giving.

❖ ❖ ❖

This love that we have
needs constant giving,
and as we give away,
it gets replenished
from His Infinite Source.
But if you refuse to give love,
the stagnant love in your own heart
putrifies and the crawling worms
start eating up your own heart!

❖ ❖ ❖

Cease to give love,
we cease to have love;
this is the strict law of love.

At all times, send out
thoughts of love to all;
kindness to all;
blessings to all.
Soon you will find
all, including your enemies,
showering you with love.

❖ ❖ ❖

But generally, your hearts are not open
for love to gush into you.
And the door of your heart
ever remains closed.
Nobody other than you
can ever throw it open,
for the door of your heart
cannot be locked from outside;
and it can be opened
only from within.

Swami Sivananda on Love

- ❖ Real communion is possible only when your heart is filled with universal love.
- ❖ Your duty is to treat everybody with love, as a manifestation of the Lord.
- ❖ Separation from beloved objects leads to suffering.
- ❖ The world is in flames, pure divine love alone can quench this flame.

- ❖ The love of wisdom yearns for knowledge as a cure from ignorance, which clings to man.
- ❖ Truth, love, beauty and goodness are one.
- ❖ Love is the ultimate reality.
  Love is the key to every problem.
  Love is the key to open the door to realms of eternal bliss.
- ❖ God's beauty is love, and His love is supreme beauty.
  Love is a great binding force.

True love is the greatest power on earth.

❖ Cultivate pure divine love for:

Love unites

Love leads

Love saves

Love elevates

Love purifies.

❖ He who plants kindness gathers love.

❖ Mistake not sentimentality for love.

❖ When you love God, you love everything.

- ❖ When you love God, the entire world becomes dear to you.
- ❖ Love the inner spiritual life.
  Love peace and silence.
  Love solitude.
  Love all, embrace all.
  Be kind to all.
- ❖ Love and work are the balance wheels of man's being.
- ❖ The mightiest force in the world is the silent power of love.

- Love neither judges nor condemns anyone.
- Love knows no reward.
  Love knows no fear.
- Love does not stand in need of proof because it itself, is a proof.

J. Krishnamurti on Love

✢ To most of us when we say we love somebody, we mean we possess that person. From possession arises jealousy, fear of losing him or her and all the conflicts. Surely such possession is not love. To be sentimental, emotional and weeping for somebody is not love.

✢ Love is like a strong flowing river. It nourishes and waters everything that comes in its way. Nothing can spoil love, for all things are dissolved in it—the good and the bad, the ugly and the beautiful. It is the only thing that is its own eternity.

✢ How little we know of love's vastness, its deathlessness, its unfathomability. To love is to be aware of eternity. We want to make relationships crude, hard and manageable. So it loses its fragrance, its beauty. All this arises because one does not love, for in it there has to be complete abandonment of oneself.

Rabindranath Tagore on Love

I seem to have loved you in numberless forms, numberless times.

In life after life, in age after age, forever. My being spellbound has made and remade the necklace of songs that you take as a gift, wear round your neck in your many forms.

In life after life, in age after age, forever.

Today it is heaped at your feet, it has found its end in you.

The love of all man's days both past and forever; universal joy, universal sorrow, universal life.

The memories of all loves merging with this one love of ours.

And the songs of every poet, past and forever.

Through love, bitter becomes sweet.
Through love, bits of copper are made gold.
Through love, stings are as honey
Through love, lions are harmless as mice.
Through love, sickness is health.
Through love, wrath is mercy.
Through love, dead rise to life.
Through love, the king becomes a slave.

— *A Persian Poem*

God is the Source of all Love

The person who serves is the person served. You serve yourself when you serve another. You serve another because his suffering causes you anguish and by relieving it, you want to save yourself from that anguish. Unless you have the anguish, your service will be hollow and insincere.

Seva (service) may be small. You may not get a chance to partake in some gigantic scheme of service through which millions may be benefited. You can lift a lame lamb over a stile, or lead a blind child across a busy road, or wipe a tear from a sick person in hospital by assuring him of your love, affection and service. That too is an act of worship which God accepts lovingly.

God will not ask you what *Seva* you did. He will ask, with what motive you did it. You may weigh the *Seva* and boast of its quantity, but God seeks quality, the purity of the mind.

Neither, performance of austerities, nor pilgrimage to all holy places, nor study of all *Sastras* (Holy Books), nor immersion in *Japa* (Prayers), will ever help one to cross the Ocean of *Samsara* (cycle of birth and death). The only path that will help you to be liberated from *Samsara* is dedicating yourself to the service of others.

Forms of worship, or the style of address may vary, but all religions are directed towards the same consummation. The same blood circulates in the limbs of everybody.

The same divine stream activates the entire universe. Visualise the Supreme Architect, that incomprehensible Designer, the unseen Lifegiver. This is spoken of as the realisation of the fatherhood of God and Brotherhood of Man.

The desire to know God, to love God and be loved by God is not a desire that binds. When awareness of God dawns in all its splendour, every worldly sensual desire is reduced to ashes in the flames of that awareness.

God is the source of all love. Through love you can emerge from the ocean of sorrow. Love for God loosens worldly bonds, saves man from the torment of birth and death.

The basis of a teacher's *sadhana* is love. Only when there is a close relationship of selfless love between the teacher and the students, and right education is imparted from the heart, that knowledge will blossom into wisdom.

The teacher dedicates himself to a great spiritual discipline when he enters this profession. He himself has to be what he advises the pupils to be. The tender minds in the classroom, are easily moulded by his example.

❖ ❖ ❖

As the air we breathe is of God's creation and available to all, so the awareness of God and his power and mercy has to be available to all. True seekers on the spiritual path must hold on to this wide outlook and on to the universality of this message. Then the conflict between disparate faiths and credos disappears by itself, and peace and love will be restored on earth.

Diversities in attitude and practices are natural and ought to be welcomed. There is no need for an iron clad hard faith. There is no place for one overall faith. Rivalry among those following different faiths cannot bring peace nor prosperity to any country.

— *Sri Sathya Sai Baba*

 Love is God.
Where love is,
there God certainly is.
Love more and more people.
Love them more and more intensely;
transform the love into service,
Transform the service into worship,
That is the highest discipline in
spirituality.

Love as thought is Truth.
Love as action is Dharma.
Love as feeling is Peace.
Love as understanding is Ahimsa.
— *Sri Sathya Sai Baba*

Love
gives and forgives.
Self
gets and forgets.

❖ ❖ ❖

Faith is the essential
sustaining force for Love

❖ ❖ ❖

— *Swami Visdudha
Chaitanya Brahmchari*

Sri Aurobindo on Love

"Love" expresses something more intense than goodwill which includes mere liking or affection. But whether love or goodwill, human feelings are always either based on or strongly mixed with ego, — hence it cannot be absolutely pure.

It is said in the Upanishads "One does not love the wife for the sake of the wife", (or the child or friend etc., as the case may be) "but for one's own self one loves the wife". There is usually the hope of return, or benefit or advantage of some kind, or of certain pleasures and gratifications, mental or physical that the person loved, can give. Remove these things and the love very soon sinks, diminishes or disappears or turns into anger, reproach, indifference or even hatred.

❖ ❖ ❖

But there is also an element of habit, something that makes the presence of the person loved a sort of necessity because it has always been there — and this is something so strong that in spite of incompatibility of temper, fierce antagonism, something like hatred, love lasts, and even these gulfs of discord are not enough to make the person part. In some cases, this feeling is not strong enough and after a time one gets accustomed to separation or accepts a substitute.

There is again, often, the element of some kind of spontaneous attraction or affinity —mental, vital or physical, which gives a stronger cohesion to love.

Lastly, there is in the highest or deepest kind of love the psychic element which comes from the inmost heart and soul, a kind of inner union of self-giving or at least a seeking for that, a tie or an urge independent of other conditions or elements, existing for its own sake and not for any mental, vital or physical pleasure, satisfaction, interest or habit.

But usually, the psychic element in human love, even where it is present, is so mixed, overloaded and hidden under other emotions that it has little chance of fulfilling itself or achieving its own natural purity and fullness.

What is called love is therefore, sometimes one thing, sometimes another, most often a confused mixture, and it is impossible to give a general answer to the many questions one wants to ask about love. It all depends on the persons and the circumstances.

When love is directed towards the Divine, there is still an ordinary human element in it. There is the need for reciprocation, and if reciprocation does not seem to come, love may sink; there is self-interest, a demand that the Divine as a giver of all that the human being wants should reciprocate, and if the demands are not acceded to, loss of faith, loss of fervour, naturally follows.

But true love for the Divine is in its fundamental nature not of this kind, but psychic and spiritual. The psychic element is the need of the inmost being for self-giving, love, adoration, union, which can only be fully satisfied by the Divine. The spiritual element is the need of the being for contact, merging, a union with its own highest and whole self, the Divine. These are two sides of the same thing.

The mind can be the support and recipient of this love, but it can be that fully, only when it becomes remoulded in harmony with the psychic and spiritual elements of the being and no longer brings in the lower insistences of the ego.

The Mother on Love

The movement of love is not limited to human beings and it is perhaps less destroyed in other worlds than in the human. Look at the flowers and trees. When the sun sets and all becomes silent, sit down for a moment and put yourself into communion with Nature; you will feel rising from the earth, from below the roots of the trees, the aspiration of an intense love and longing, — a longing for something that is gone and a wish to have it back again. There is a yearning so pure and intense that if you can feel the movement in the trees, your own being will also go up in an ardent prayer for the peace and light and love that are unmanifested here.

Love is universal and eternal; it is always manifesting itself and always identical in its essence. It is a Divine Force; for the distortions we see in its apparent workings, belong to its instruments. Love does not manifest itself in human beings alone; it is everywhere. Its movement is there in plants, perhaps in every stone; in animals, it is easy to detect its presence. All the deformations of this great and Divine Power come from ignorance and selfishness.

Love, the eternal force, has no clinging, no desire, no hunger for possession, no self-regarding attachment; it is, in its pure movement, the seeking of a union for the self with the Divine, Love Divine gives itself and asks for nothing.

What human beings have made of it, we need not say; they have turned it into an ugly and repulsive thing. And yet, even in human beings, the first contact with love does bring in something of its purer substance; they become capable, for a moment, of forgetting themselves, for a moment its divine touch awakens and magnifies all that is fine and beautiful.

❖ ❖ ❖

But afterwards there comes to the surface the human nature, full of its impure demands, asking for something in exchange, bartering what it gives, clamouring for its own inferior satisfaction, distorting and soiling what was divine.

❖ ❖ ❖

Love between human beings, in all its forms, the love of parents for children and of children for parents, of brothers and sisters, of friends and lovers, is all tainted with ignorance, selfishness and all the other defects which are man's ordinary drawbacks.

So, instead of completely ceasing to love— which is very difficult, as Sri Aurobindo says, and which would simply dry up the heart and serve no end — one must learn how to love better: to love with devotion, with self-giving, self-abnegation, and to struggle, not against love itself, but against its distorted forms: against all forms of monopolising, of attachment, possessiveness, jealousy, and all the feelings which accompany these main movements. Not to want to possess, to dominate; and not to want to impose one's will, one's whims, one's desires; or to want to take, to receive, but to *give;* not to insist on the other's response, but be content with one's *own love;* not to seek one's personal interest and joy and the fulfilment of one's personal desire, but to be satisfied with the giving of one's love and affection; and not to ask for any response. Simply to be happy to love — nothing more.

❖ ❖ ❖

If you do that, you have taken a giant stride forward and can, through this attitude, gradually advance farther in the feeling itself, and realise one day that love is not something personal, that love is a universal divine feeling which manifests itself through you more or less finely, but which in its essence is something divine.

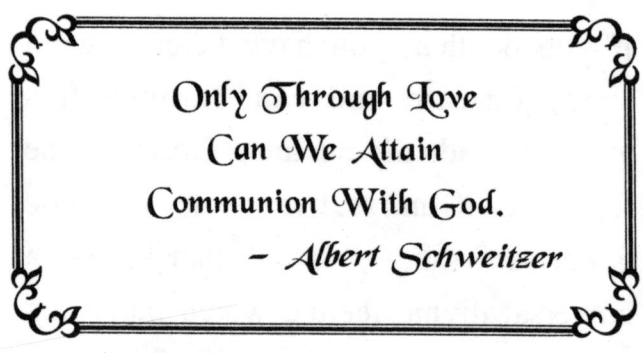

Even three times a day to offer
three hundred cooking pots of food
does not match a portion of the merit
acquired in One instant of love.
- *Nagarjuna Precious Garland 283*

Love
All Beings As Yourself

Love is the oil
you put in
the lamp of knowledge.
— Reverend Ma

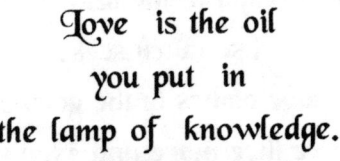

We can do no great things.
Only small things
with great love.
— Mother Teresa

I love thee more
Because thou chose to smile
Even when I suffer, even when I stumble,
Giving me the foretaste of a distant bliss
A pre-vision of the beauty's moon
I so much seek.
Thy message comes in the garb of misery,
To love thee more and even more.
From the heart of grief issues
a spring of joy,
From the timidity's cage comes out
a bird of courage,
A calm fortitude is my love's reward.

— Sri Aurobindo

Love is a Many Splendoured Thing

Love is the quintessence of happy human relationships.

Its manifestation extends beyond human beings—to both living and non-living things.

In its highest form, it is Divinity itself.

In fact, Love is God and God is love.

Love is undoubtedly the most powerful gift of God which must form the basis of all our daily activities.

If contentment is the ultimate objective of life, love is the easiest path leading to it.

Service to humanity is the surest method to achieve it.

Compassion and forgiveness are two essential attributes of a loving nature.

So, love all, always.

Love and Compassion

The greatest degree of inner tranquillity comes from the development of love and compassion.

The more we care for the happiness of others, the greater our own sense of well-being becomes. Cultivating a close, warm-hearted feeling for others automatically puts the mind at ease. This helps remove whatever fears or insecurities we may have and gives us the strength to cope with any obstacles we encounter. It is the ultimate source of success. The need for love lies at the very foundation of human existence. It results from the profound inter-dependence we all share with one another.

The Medicine of Altruism

In Tibet, they say that many illnesses can be cured by the medicine of love and compassion. These are the ultimate source of human happiness, and our need for them lies at the very core of our being. Unfortunately, love and compassion have been omitted from many spheres of social interaction. Usually confined to family and home, their practice in public life is considered impractical, even naive. This is tragic.

The practice of compassion is not just a symptom of unrealistic idealism but the most effective way to pursue the best interests of others as well as our own. The more we— as a nation, a group or as individuals — depend upon others, the more it is in our best interest to ensure their well-being.

Practising altruism is the real source of compromise and cooperation; merely recognising our need for harmony is not enough. A mind committed is like an overflowing reservoir — a constant source of energy, determination and kindness. It gives rise to many good qualities, such as forgiveness, tolerance, inner strength and the confidence to overcome fear and insecurity. The compassionate mind is like an elixir; it is capable of transforming bad situations into beneficial ones.

Therefore, we should not limit our expressions of love and compassion to our family and friends. Nor is compassion only the responsibility of clergy, health care and social workers. It is the necessary business of every part of the human community.

— *The Dalai Lama*

Conquer anger by love.
— Dhammapada 223

❖ ❖ ❖

Let a man overcome anger by love,
let him overcome evil through good,
let him overcome the greedy with liberty,
a liar by truth.
— Anon

❖ ❖ ❖

Hatred never ceases by hatred.
By love alone it ceases.
This is an ancient law.

— The Buddha

"Power based on love
is a thousand times more
effective and permanent than the one
derived from fear of punishment."
— *Mahatma Gandhi*

The feeling of true love
arises from purity;
a purity wherein
there are no distinctions
and demarcations.
— *Parthasarathy*

Triangle of Love

- ❖ *Para-Bhakti* has three important features, which may be termed as the three angles of love. These are :
- ♦ Love seeks no return; for it is the nature of pure love to give, and not to take or demand.
- ♦ Love knows no fear; for they are incompatible. Fear is the result of narrow self-centredness, based on the physical form and its own welfare. In true love the devotee surrenders

himself completely to Him and feels himself to be a part and parcel of Him. There is no place for fear in such a state of mind.

- Love knows no rival; for in it is embodied the devotee's highest ideal.

Bhavas of Love

- ❖ To channelise human affections into forms of love for God is known as the Bhavas. These Bhavas are classified as follows:
- ◆ *Santa* or placid and philosophical, without much of a personal element in it.
- ◆ *Dasya* or attitude of a servant.
- ◆ *Apatya* or attitude of a son to a father.
- ◆ *Sakhya* or relation of a friend towards a friend.

- *Vatsalya* or affection of a parent towards a child.
- *Madhura* or sweet, which can take the form of pure conjugal love or of illegitimate love between a lover and sweetheart.

Love: Concept of Supreme Consciousness

❖ The emotion is the same in both the higher and the lower kinds of love. When we direct our love towards a higher, a more inspiring ideal, our minds expand, our faculties broaden, our vision deepens and our efficiencies multiply. When the emotion of love goes towards external objects of pleasure, things or beings, it slowly shells us into a life of tensions and anxieties, into a prison of sorrows and excitements, pangs and sobs. It is then that we really "fall" in love!

❖ We "rise" in love when love is true and dynamic and there is a great joy felt in giving love rather than meekly hoping to receive. Love is its own reward. To give love is true freedom, to demand love is pure slavery.

❖ Love is the highest moral truth and hence "love thyself" is the greatest moral injunction if the seeker does not misunderstand the advice. It does not mean loving the body or obeying the mind meekly. The mind and intellect are gross matter envelopments that have come to seemingly limit the illimitable Supreme Consciousness which is the real Self in all of us. When the seeker's mind melts in the warmth of his single-minded love for God, the Self in us, the sublime fusion of the finite with the Infinite takes place.

Love the Spirit of Service

❖ The noblest service we can do is that which we render unselfishly, quickly, silently, without any expectation of gratitude or reward.

❖ The spirit of service must spring from our Love, and so during service, our heart expands and we learn to watch the gurgling flood of love swelling in its onward gush from us. With this deepened and widened sense of charity, mercy, kindness and good will to all, our heart opens out, and a seeker who contemplates from such a heart bursting with love alone can climb to the highest within himself.

— *Swami Chinmayananda*

True Love

- ❖ Sacrifice and service are two essential elements of true love.

- ❖ True love leads to total dedication and ultimate surrender. It has no demands and no preconditions. It is not necessarily a two-way traffic, nor a commercial contract between two parties. True love is indeed complete, absolute and total.

- ❖ True love is greatly dependent on unshakeable faith. Doubts and suspicion have no place in true love. Grouses and complaints do not exist in relationships based on true love. There are no expectations in true love as it thrives on giving and not expecting anything in return.

❖ Thus, true love will lead one to divine love — for God is indeed love and love is God.

— *Anandi Didi (Yogi Divine Society)*

Love
is the basis of happiness
in the world.

Love and Knowledge

❖ In the highest state of devotion the lover loses himself in the Beloved and attains the state of non-duality. Thus the highest form of knowledge and the highest form of devotion are one and the same in the end, though at the disciplinary stage, they may differ. Love and knowledge are thus the obverse and the reverse of the same coin even as *Personal Iswara* and *Impersonal Brahman* are.

❖ So when a man has this love in him, he becomes eternally blessed, eternally happy.

— *Swami Vivekananda*